Poems

FOR THE
STOCKING

thoughts

FOR THE
HEART

First published 2010

ISBN No: 978-1-907636-11-0

Published by Verité CM Ltd

Cover design, typesetting and production management by
Verité CM Ltd, Worthing, West Sussex UK
+44 (0) 1903 241975

Printed in England

Introduction

Thank you dear reader for picking up this book,
you may have bought it or you may have been given
it as a gift, you may even be flicking through its' pages in a
bookshop!!! However it came to be in your possession,
it is my hope that you enjoy what you read!

The book is a collection of selected poems that I have written to
reflect the impression that certain situations have had on me, we
are all affected by our surroundings in one way or another, by the
people we meet and simply by life itself… as we see it.

I hope you will smile at some poems, I also hope some
of them will touch your heart, perhaps some will prompt you to
write a few verses for yourself!!

Now, go and make a nice cup of tea or coffee, sit in your favourite
chair and even put your feet up while you sit (difficult to do if you
are in a bookshop!) and read, out
loud, a poem or two…

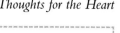

Contents

The following poem was written as a mother who wants to provide a good meal at Christmas for friends and family alike, knowing that her oven is rather inadequate for the job! Hence the title! It is a true reflection of actual occurrences and at the time of printing, almost twelve months later… the cooker remains the same! Many cooker 'repairers' have visited the home over this period… strangely enough they can never find ANYTHING wrong with it!

Three Rings on my Cooker!

'Five Gold Rings'… the Christmas song rings out…
But I've got only three… and it makes me want to shout!!

As Advent marches on… and days to Christmas whizzing by
My well planned Christmas cooking plans bring tears
to each brown eye.

In stately palaces and humble flats, up and down the land
The Christmas 'cooks' already, have their menus loosely planned.

They'll be working to precision. Timing… calling all the shots
But me, I only have three rings! And an abundance, it seems of pots!

I'll need one ring for the gravy, one for the brussel sprouts
Another for carrot and turnip, delaying the poor pudding no doubts!

For my cookers' sought to fail me! Indeed in my finest hour!
As one ring isn't working! It's failing in its' power.

I've tried to have the ring repaired… But there's no part to replace
And so it's just not working… And the menu's in disgrace!!

What can a mother do? When she's one ring short of a cooker?
Juggle all the various pans? A mish mash, to any onlooker.

Well, I have learned a lesson
After cooking thirty or more Christmas dinners
… and that's around the Christmas table…
there's no losers and no winners…
The 'DINNER' will be 'perfect'
Whether undercooked or burned…
As 'nothing' can really ruin it…
That's the lesson I have learned!

A meal… prepared in love, shared with family and friends
Matters not about the food… but the message that it sends.
So… it's… three rings… again… this Christmas.
I won't be fussed or fraught
I'll do my best under the circumstance,
and enjoy the day as I ought!

Jackie Doherty 2010

This next poem was written following a conversation with a young child who didn't know anything about God or Jesus and had only ever used the words as a swear word, which left me wondering who he would turn to...

Dearest Father Christmas...

Dearest Father Christmas, I hope you get this letter…
I send you lots and lots of love and hope Rudolph's nose is better.
I thank you for the toys last year, you kindly gave to me
And understand the reason there was no bike beneath the tree.
I even understand, you simply can't be everywhere
And this letter to you now is really a little prayer…

I don't know who to turn to, who else would really care?
And since I wrote last Christmas, we've had a real bad year.
My daddy went to prison, and one that's far away
I don't know how to contact him and think of him each day.
My mummy has no money and cries most of the time
She says we are the victims of my daddy's alleged crime.

Other children speak of gramps and grans, but I don't think
that I have any…
There's no brothers, sisters, aunties… but my uncles they are many.

Dearest Father Christmas… I heard about God in school
I heard He longs to help us and loves us as a rule.
Could you send God to me this Christmas? Could you get this
message to Him?
Before we fall into despair, our lives to rack and ruin?
It's Christmas Eve, I'm on my own… There's no tree here this year
But I believe in you, Santa Claus, and know you'll read my prayer.

"Love came down at Christmas" we sang in school one day
So just tell God we need Him please… As God is 'love' they say…

I don't know how He'll help us…
But He'll know… of that I'm sure
So give a bike to someone else…
Not me… I need much more.
THANK YOU.

Jackie Doherty 2010

I had been watching the early morning news which showed awful scenes following the Haiti earthquake in January 2010. At home, we were experiencing severe weather conditions and as I viewed from the comfort of my living room, they were showing desperate people trying to take the emergency supplies, this was over and above what had been provided to them, my heart went out to them and it brought to mind what I had witnessed myself, that very morning in my own back garden! I had been laying out food for the birds, lots of it… but the fat birds wouldn't let the little birds near… at all! It was the survival of the fattest!! I then sat and penned this reflection.

Emergency Supplies

Emergency supplies, have been dished up…
And served to their own feeding site
There's enough… to feed each hungry mouth
As their hunger and thirsts really bite

Each 'meal' has been measured and chosen
To maintain good health and nutrition
Supplies will be given as needed
There's no need for this nasty derision
All hungry! I know who can blame them!
They may think this could be their last meal
I wish I could speak in their language
To gently explain how I feel…

"There's no need to push, fight or bite back
No need for the bully to stand guard!
Please don't scare away the young thin ones!
I'm finding this sight really hard!"
It's not a roaring hot desert abroad…
Nor a war zone that begs for a pardon…
Not a famine scene up on our screens…
But the birds! In my very own garden!!

The snow's falling thick and quite deep
It's winter, crisp, even and crude
The birds make a swoop for some shelter
And hustle and fight for the food!!
They arrive in all different sizes
But I see to my horror and dismay
The fattest eat first… till they're full
And they chase the young, small birds away!!

I wonder with awe how they're 'living' at all.
Even the fatter ones… so tiny it seems
How on earth can their thin legs sustain them?
In this winter of minus degrees…
As it's grab, grab and grab in the malls…
in nature it's grab, grab, grab… also too.
There it is… that old 'pecking order'…
and about it… there's nought we can do!

Jackie Doherty 2010

Christmas always bring back childhood
memories, the halcyon days, and among
those memories, none are clearer than
those of my mother...

My Mother Loved People At Christmas Time

My Mother Loved People…
    My Mother Loved…
        My Mother…

Who of us can face Christmas…
Without remembering Christmases past?
The traditions we learned in our childhood
And the memories made… ones that last…

I have so many such memories, that return to me year upon year
But none as vivid as my mother, whose heart was filled up
with good cheer.
She savoured the essence of 'Christmas' kept it true in her heart
all year long
She taught us to look out for our neighbours, especially ones
who don't 'belong'

Our house would be 'home' for the stranger, with a welcome
for each waif and stray
A hot meal, a bed, a listening ear, was just part of her being each day.

And Christmas would be no exception,
As ordered chaos, for me seemed to be
With no presents wrapped nor veggies prepared…
Which caused me angst to a certain degree

I worried about 'setting the table'… I stressed over 'things'
not yet 'done'
Whilst my mother would fuss over people, would laugh…
would love… would have fun.

And I've learned in the years that ensued… As my tables been 'set' to a T!
My presents all wrapped to perfection… and the house spick and span
as can be…

I've learned that I'd rather have chaos… I've learned to just 'open'
the home
I've learnt to offer a welcome… to any who are living alone.

What's the use of having everything 'perfect' when there's no joy or
fun in the air?
Where's the sense in 'shutting out' neighbours? How did we grow
not to care?

So, this Christmas I set you a challenge…
to invite someone round you don't love!
Fuss over them, feed them, show joy, welcome them in…
in GOD'S LOVE
It's very easy to love those we like,
to give when we think we'll be repaid
But Jesus tells us to love our enemies.
You may have read this but have you obeyed?

So, I try to remember my mother, who loved with a simple pure heart
Who sought out her neighbours to love them and made such a
difference for their part.
I'll try to remember the fun, to recall the joy felt by all
As I emulate mother this Christmas and step up to the plate of His call.

"Love your neighbour" as yourself
"Love your enemies" too!
Forgive, forgive, forgive again!
Bless (even) those who'd curse you.

My mother…
        My mother loved…
                My mother loved people…
                        My mother loved people at Christmastime.

Jackie Doherty 2010

I had been watching the news, it portrayed the 'homecoming' of a Regiment, showing the men returning from active service in Afghanistan, being reunited with loved ones, parents, sweethearts, children, sisters, brothers, husbands and wives. The cameras rolled as personnel entered the gymnasium for the long awaited welcome home. The following is an account of what I felt watching this heart touching homecoming...

Homecoming

I watched it on the news, in fact several times across the day
It was a Regiments' homecoming, televised…
it made me bow my head to pray

I cried… who wouldn't, moved to tears the cameras rolling on
Couples kissing, hugging… tight, till my eyes focused on one…

Some men were fumbling, patting kids
Kissing wives and embracing mothers
Gently tweaking babies' cheeks
Hand shaking with the others…

Battle-scarred, perhaps Battle-scared
The men returned to base
And what seemed unspoken in their voice
Was written clearly on their face.

But there it was… I caught it
As the camera rolled on by
A young wife 'waiting'… patiently
And her demeanour made me cry.

I thought I'd spotted something
Right there on that young face
That… I… had felt so many times
In another time… another place

Her husband enveloped the children
He hugged and kissed them each
But he'd left his wife just standing
Awkwardly… out of his reach

Her eyes just told it all
How she yearned to feel his breath
So grateful for his safe return
Escaping loss of limb and death

She'd wait… this was the kid's time
She wouldn't, couldn't intervene
But within her breast lay a yearning
Which her husband hadn't seen.

She too was Battle-scarred
She too was Battle-scared
As she'd fought her way on home ground
With dignity, pride… and for eventualities… prepared.

And now they would have to work hard
To come together as a pair
To share and shoulder everyday life
And to nurture the babes in their care.

The news blurted on in the background
As my mind and its' thoughts were now racing
I wondered of people who were struggling
With troubles which they too were facing

We don't have to have been in a war zone
To feel beaten or indeed Battle-scarred
Sometimes the problems people suffer
Are there in their own back yard.

We don't have to have been in a war zone
To feel crushed or indeed Battle-scared
And many live out their lives like this…
… living a life that's impaired.

But one day…
We too will have a special 'Homecoming'
Where there'll be no awkward standing around
Nor will there be tears or heartache…
Just joy… and real love will abound.

Jackie Doherty 2010

25

Although this next poem was written well over twenty years ago, I can remember writing it! I had been aware, probably for the first time, that Jesus had been born in an animal shelter!! I'm still amazed at this thought! There was no room anywhere for Him to be born in that busy place. Today many people are so busy they have no room for Him in their busy lives

No Room Here

It's so strange – I often have wondered
That for God's Son – there was no room in the inn
That He came amid basic beginnings
A place lowly and humble within

Why! That's no place for God's Son to be born!
And it's always a puzzle as to why…
An animal's shelter should house Him
When He'd the splendour of the heavenly sky

No, no room in the inn, then for Jesus
But who was bothered? Who knew who He was?
Who'd imagine His birth was significant?
Not to mention His death on the cross.

But nothing ever changes
There's no room in men's hearts still today
Life's too busy, such a rush, there's no time
To think, understand or to pray

This same Jesus can't enter man's 'Inn'
Until it is humble and lowly
And then He imparts understanding
Albeit sometimes rather slowly

I needn't have wondered so long
It's all there in the Bible to read
That He longs to dwell inside each of us
No matter our colour or creed

He cannot dwell in a proud heart
So humble your heart from within
Don't offer the age old reply… this Christmas
Sorry… There's no room in this 'inn'

Jackie Doherty 1989

It was December last year, I was walking through a pretty town, hurrying along not wanting to be outdoors a moment longer than I needed to! Despite being wrapped up for the cold weather I was cold and hungry, I took a short cut through a church courtyard and the bells suddenly and unexpectedly rang out, I looked around and spotted someone sat on the floor with his back against the church wall, he looked very sad indeed, in tattered clothes, he was half clutching a half full, half empty bottle of alcohol... I have never forgotten his look of despair and wrote this upon my return...

The Bells Ring Out

The bells ring out, I hear them
They're loud and clear and shrill
Becoming quieter and softer
As I reel from my latest 'thrill'

The Bells rang out in days gone by
When I was just a boy
When innocence was all I knew
With only good things to enjoy

When did it change? When will it change?
As all becomes a blur
An addict now is what I am
And who is left to care?

Oh! Jesus!… Can you hear me? I'm sick
Oh! Jesus!… Can you heal me? I'm tired
I'm sick and tired of being sick and tired
Jesus, can you heal me?!

No friends left, no family to care
No Christmas, no Christmas dinner
Yet I once heard and knew a man
Who loves each and every sinner

Can He heal me now… as the bells ring out
Can He hear me now… as I cry out
Will He help me… as I dry out
Will He love me now… within… without.

Jackie Doherty

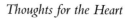

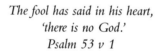

The fool has said in his heart,
'there is no God.'
Psalm 53 v 1

How could you not believe?

"How can you believe?… " people ask me…
"It's garbage, no creator exists!
There's no master plan, there's no Jesus!
You're deluding yourself." He insists.

But just today, sat quietly alone
Having coffee in the warm winter sun
A beautiful car drove quite near me
And I heard the faint voice of someone…

"Wow ! What a fantastic car!
The designer must be proud of his plan
To design such a fantastic model
To be driven around for mere man!"

I smiled to myself as I heard this
… the car just didn't 'appear'
People accept there's a designer for 'things'
But not for creation I fear!

And just then, came a bird to my table.
It sang an indecipherable tweet
And I watched it, in awe of its' designer
As it hopped and then stopped at my feet.

I compared my own legs to this birdies'
Marvelling that each had their use
The 'right' feet were on the 'right' creature!
My imagination began then to muse…

As soon as the bird hopped away
An ant was approaching quite near
And I carefully observed every movement
His whole being caused me to stare…

The flowers that sat in the vase
A work of indefinable beauty
Awakened a sense of amazement
For the designers' outstanding ingenuity.

I was 'struck' by 'His' world… all around me
Even there in the fast moving street
There were tell tale signs of His presence
As grass burst forth through the concrete

In awe at all I had noticed
My eyes moved up to the clouds
Where I pondered and gazed at the skyline
Now unaware of the crowds.

So, tell me there's no creator, no God!
Tell me it just all 'came to exist'
Tell me… your body had no designer
Quite the opposite… I'd have to insist.

Jackie Doherty 2010

Many years ago now (1982) when I invited Jesus into my heart, I felt it of utmost importance that my old Sunday School Teacher should know that I had, after years of going to church, now 'understood' and that I'd made a decision to be a 'believer' and wanted a personal relationship with God. I was living in another country at the time and didn't know if my old Sunday Schoolteacher was dead or alive! I telephoned my mother long distance and asked her if she knew whether or not… well, I wrapped it up more appropriately than that! And yes, my mother knew where she was living! I asked my mother to seek her out for me and that I felt it necessary that she should know my decision! My mother passed on my messages and later relayed to me how pleased she had been to have heard the news and that I had bothered to seek her out.

When I visited my mother some time later, it was my intention to pay her a visit myself to thank her for her instruction and more importantly to thank her for praying for me, which I strongly believe she had done for years, sadly, there was no opportunity to do so as she had passed away shortly after my mother visited her.

This is written in her memory and for all the faithful Sunday School Teachers everywhere.

The Sunday School Teacher

No one ever really sees the sacrifices made.
No one ever really knows the things that they would rather…
And no one even really cares
Except of course…
      'the Father'

He sees the things you do for Him. He sees your high ambition
He even sees your motives. He sees your heart condition…
      'our Father'

Each week by week they minister. To the children in their care
Praying, loving, nurturing. In the hope that they too would hear…
      'their Father'

Sometimes, never, even knowing. If they've helped a child along
As they relay His 'words'. In play, in games, in song…
      'words of the Father'

They can only do their bit in faith, God's spirit will do the rest
To nurture and nourish a childs' heart, for a lifetime that can be
blessed…

       'by the Father'

So teach them that HE loves them, each and every one
In troubles and in years ahead, that's what they'll call upon.
As I did… once I knew the truth, as my heart was changed inside
From head knowledge into heart knowledge, my spiritual eyes
were open wide.
From tiny seeds sown at Sunday School, From my 'teachers'
fervent prayer
I knew at once when I believed that I had to contact her…

… To tell her I was now a Christian, not a church- goer as before
I asked my mother to track her down and she told her at her door.

Jackie Doherty

2010 was a year of contrasts weather wise! Snow like we'd never seen in years, incredible rainfall! Scorching temperatures… on a hot July day I was creeping about the garden trying to keep out of the searing heat when all of a sudden…

43

Where on Earth did that Come from?

It's difficult to imagine the setting!
A most beautiful day in July
The heat had been so overpowering,
when it came… a storm in the sky!
In fact I had just been complaining
'Oh it's hot, I can't bear it much longer!'
When all hell was let loose in a moment…
and the effects of the storm were much stronger!
I'd been creeping around in the shadows.
To avoid the heat and the sun
Wearing little and moving so slowly,
then it came… then the storm begun.
In a flash (or even quicker) it grew dark
And the wind blew large branches from trees
Everything was blowing around me
It was more than a very strong breeze.
In two minutes the day was so changed!
The garden resembled a mess
Ambulances screamed in the background
And people were scared I confess
It reminded me so of our lives…
how often when all's going well..
We'll be hit with the biggest of problems-
When they'll come we just never can tell.
In just a few minutes of raging…
Computers and trees were all 'down'

One tree had smashed through a roof…
devastation was seen all around.
We can pass through the seasons unscathed
And then happen upon troubles and strife
And although God's there in the detail…
He never promised a smooth easy life!
We can complain (as I did) about sunshine
Yet, what awaited, unknown, was much worse!
Instead we should always be grateful
In all circumstances…
though the very idea sounds perverse.
To give THANKS for troubles and hardship?
To be grateful, feel joy in the sorrow!?
Sounds madness itself… some would say
Never knowing what could come by tomorrow!!
In the end… (the beginning and the middle)
God alone… controls weather and seasons
And to we mortal men, who's as dust
There's no reason for Him to give reasons!
So, for… whatever… that crosses your path.
Just live it… give thanks anyway
Be reverent,… in awe of the creator.
As He PROMISES to be with you each day!

We can praise Him in the storm…

Jackie Doherty 12th July 2010

*Many of us, or some of our loved ones, are
cared for by nurses from time to time and
mostly the experience is a positive one.
Most nurses have an altruistic manner,
often going beyond the realm of duty,
putting into practice 'something' that can't
be defined in a job description, but they too
have 'a life'. Who cares for the carer?*

The Nurse

Problems at home
Emotionally drained
Too many shifts
Physically strained…
        as she goes… in the strength of the Lord

Yet no one would know
Even less… there's no one to care
As she carries on 'nursing'
Spreading joy here and there…
        as she works in the strength of the Lord

Once in her uniform
Once in her shoes
Once she's on duty
Her worries she'll lose…
        as she loves in the strength of the Lord

More than just meeting the deadlines
Much more than the targets she's reaching
She puts into practice God's commandment
She puts into practice Christ's teaching…
                    as she gives in the strength of the Lord

At the end of the day in reflection
She recalls all the ones in her care
The patients, their families, her colleagues
And lifts them all up in a prayer…
                    as she rests in the strength of the Lord

Jackie Doherty 2010

When it's almost Christmas…
my thoughts go out to any parent who
is dreading Christmas because they
have no job…

Dad on the Dole

I can't go home… can't face them! As they ask again in vain
"Any luck today then?"… But I can't stay in the rain.
The library is closing, my clothes are all soaked through
There's no money for a coffee and my shoes are leaking too.

So home it is… with heavy heart, can't bear to see their faces
It's only weeks to Christmas. Soaked, I quicken up my paces
This time last year was different, good job, good car, good life
How quickly things can turn around, no job now and a
pregnant wife.

Over thirty or more job interviews, writing here and ringing there
Grasping straws at anything and almost in despair
I'm a qualified electrician, but don't feel the brightest spark
And really I'll do any job, painter, barman… gardener in the park

I just want to earn some money! The kids need coats and shoes
My dole won't spread to luxuries, we neither smoke nor booze
There'll be no presents this year, no fancy goods or toys
No buying more than essentials unlike the other girls and boys.

But… hmm! we all will have each other! And our hearts are filled
with love
We're happy and we're healthy and our faith's in God above.
He never promised us an easy life, nor riches beyond compare…
But in times of 'lack' and 'plenty' He promises to be there…

I love my wife, she loves me, we and the kids are healthy
As I consider on these things, it makes me now feel wealthy
I can go home and face them, we'll trust, hope, love, obey
We'll stand upon His promises… and live to love another day.

Dear Lord, you've heard my cry, now strengthen me I pray
To face the unknown future, draw near to me each day.
My trust is not in silver, my worth is not in gold
My heart is in your hands… your love you won't withhold.
I trust you for my future, though all seems dark and dim
I set my mind on things above, (singing praises now to Him)

'I thank you for mixed blessings, for the hard times and the pain
I thank you that you love me, Lord, I even thank you for this
pouring rain
I'm poor, cold, broke and soaking
Yet I'm rich beyond compare
I feel your hand upon my life
Now there's no place… for despair.'

I sing the psalm out loud, the one I learnt in parrot fashion
But never before have I prayed it, with such depth, such tears,
such passion
'The Lord He is my shepherd! And I shall nothing need… "
He'll lead me where I need to be, no matter code or creed.

I quicken my pace to reach home now
And hope's replaced guilt, fear and shame
It's so strange that I feel this new purpose
Just by trusting in His powerful name…

… Mmm! The soup and the bread smell's appealing
My wife and the kids full of joy.
"We've prayed for renewal and healing" they say
Nothing… Could this moment destroy.

We sit and give thanks and we eat
And the 'worries' aren't as big as before
And before we can finish our chatting
There's a knock heard upon our front door

It's our neighbour, I'm caught by surprise
"Come in, out the rain!" I demand
"It came by mistake just this morning"
As he offers a letter by hand.

And a warmth spreads all over my being
… which I'll tell to the children one day
I fumble and open the letter…
'… Please can you start work on Monday… '

Jackie Doherty 2010

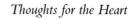

The following poem… sadly… a true story!

A Smashing Gift!

My friend had taken up flower arranging…
And I considered a gift that would suit
I selected a beautiful glass vase
It was special, so different, so cute!

I bought it in Holland especially for her,
in a florist of well known repute
I knew it would inspire her creations,
price never came into dispute.

She would love it! I knew that for sure,
it was plastic but looked just like glass
Its' potential was endless, unlimited…
few vases were in the same class!

But whenever I journeyed to see her,
I sadly forgot her new pot
And two years passed by when I realized,
ashamed and embarrassed I'd forgot!

She then had a series of setbacks,
which reminded me to send off her gift
I was saddened two years had passed by
and I'd just let the vase drift and drift.

I searched for a beautiful wrapper,
in which to post off the surprise
And selected a beautiful gold box.
Which I knew would wow her brown eyes!!

The parcel took an age to arrive,
as I waited and awaited a text
To thank me for thinking about her…
unprepared for what happened next!!

The Gold box arrived to her home…
two years and two weeks overdue
And her husband who took the delivery,
felt, something was amiss, he just knew!

She opened the welcome Gold Box…
expecting… only heaven knew what!
But for certain this was most unexpected,
something that won't be forgot!!

Two years and two weeks she had waited
For a gift that would cheer her sad eyes
And indeed it did have a wow factor
But more of a shock than surprise!!

For the Box contained such a smashing gift
And indeed it was in its' own class
As the vase was in thousands of pieces
As the plastic turned out to be glass… oops!

Jackie Doherty 2010

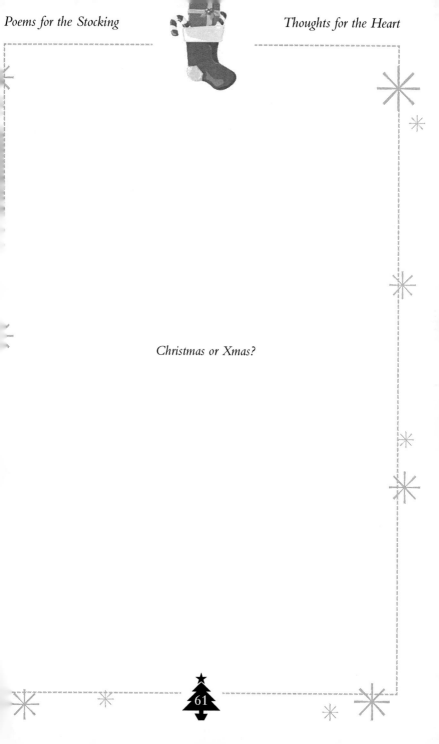

Christmas or Xmas?

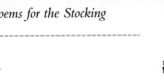

Christmas Tree or Xmas Tree

There it stands…
A feast for little eyes
A symbol of what Christmas means
The glamour and surprise
The shiny, glistening baubles
The tinsel trailing round
The smell of evergreen bush
The tinkle, tinkle sound

There it boasts…
The splendidness of light
The beauty of its being
The impression 'all is right'
The gifts beneath all perfect
The chocolates on the tree
The crackers lay awaiting for their eventuality

There it stood…
Long ago, that other tree,
No baubles, tinsel, pretty lights
Just a cross of misery
Two trees though poles apart
With Christ though a part of each
Don't leave Christ out of your Christmas
Or you'll leave Him out of reach

There it is…
For those who'll understand
The Gift from God on that tree
And the life for you He's planned
His gift's not tinsel wrapped
But the light will never fade
His gift is your salvation
And the price already paid.

Jackie Doherty

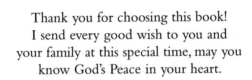

Thank you for choosing this book!
I send every good wish to you and
your family at this special time, may you
know God's Peace in your heart.

Jackie
x